A Brief History of Watnall₁

and surrounding area

J M Lee

Edition 2/2007

CONTENTS

This is the second in a series of short books concerning the history of some of the larger settlements in N W Nottingham by J M Lee

Cover Picture: Main Road and the Queen's Head, early 20th century

1 Introduction and Early Days

Watnall today is a pleasant, leafy dormitory area for a collection of nearby conurbations, including the City of Nottingham itself. It blends into similar residential areas, which stretch away seamlessly towards Kimberley, Nuthall and beyond. It is a desirable place to live, with a great pressure for modern housing. With the energy and pace of its daily life, it is unmistakably part of the outer perimeter of a major city, yet had you been here two centuries ago you would probably have been impressed by its isolation. Watnall would have been an anonymous and remote corner of rural England, with landscapes moulded over centuries of agricultural struggle. Most folk tended to come and go without much trace, yet it's possible to piece together at least something of a story which turns out to be fascinating and complex. This short account of Watnall's development over the ages starts about two thousand years ago, at the beginning of Roman times.

Early Days. The Romans occupied Britain from 43 AD until about 410 AD. There is scant evidence of their occupation in the Watnall area, although several excavated sites exist nearby. Probably the most important is a fort on the hilltop now occupied by Broxtowe estate some three miles away. This is thought to date from the first seventy or so years of the Roman occupation, when a military buffer zone was established along the line of the Trent and Severn. It seems that, for a time, the area was a vital frontier on the northern limit of Roman occupation.

When Rome collapsed, so did the stability which it brought. Throughout Europe, dangerous times set in and, on the wild northern coasts especially, warlike Germanic raiders started to cross the sea, spurred on by poverty and thoughts of plunder. The Angles and the Saxons made much use of Britain's rivers, especially the Trent, eventually settling and founding the Saxon town of Snotingham (Nottingham) upon the heights occupied by the present-day Lace Market.

By the 7th century, England's disparate collection of wild new immigrants had formed themselves into seven Anglo Saxon kingdoms, which vied with each other for supremacy. The Watnall area was part of the Kingdom of Mercia, which became dominant in the 7th century, but Mercia was supplanted in importance by Wessex after Offa died in 796.

From the early part of the 9th century, Danish raiders became increasingly troublesome off the English coast. At first their raids were isolated, but in 865 a great Danish army landed in East Anglia, and by 874 the Danes were in control of Mercia and large parts of Wessex. King Alfred fought back valiantly, and in 886 he concluded a treaty with the invaders, establishing a boundary approximately along the line of Watling Street (roughly a line between London and the Dee estuary). This puts Watnall firmly in the area which later became known as the Danelaw. The Danelaw was re-conquered by the kings of Wessex in the 10th century, but the uniqueness of Danish customs within the area was recognised and the King's new subjects were left a vast field of autonomy. Evidence still remains in the area of Danish occupation in the form of place names.

Domesday. All this early national activity eventually filtered through to mould local events in Watnall. A small settlement of some sort had arisen by the time of the Norman Conquest in 1066 as it's mentioned by name "Watenot" in the Domesday Book. This was the survey commissioned by William the Conqueror of his new English territories, won after the Battle of Hastings. It lists land ownership at two notable times: in the reign of Edward the Confessor just before William arrived, and at the time of the survey in 1086/7, twenty years after the battle. The entries in Domesday are quite confusing and open to different interpretation by different experts, but, fundamentally, before the Conquest, there were two manors in Watnall. One was owned by Grimkell and the other by Siward. The term "manor" was itself used to describe different things, but it can be interpreted simply as a unit of land ownership. Grimkell seems to have been important in that he had other holdings in both Kimberley and Newthorpe. In 1086/7, twenty years after the Conquest, two land holders are noted: Grimkell, quite possibly the man already mentioned, and Jocelyn (Gozelin).

After the Conquest, all the land locally was placed by King William under the overlordship of his great follower William de Peverel. Peverel was one of William's mightiest men, having 55 lordships, or manors, in Nottinghamshire alone. He was not locally based and would have had little if anything to do with the area himself, it would have been sub tenanted to lesser lords in the feudal fashion, but these early times are shrouded in mystery. The exact manner in which Saxon occupiers were either replaced by their Norman conquerors or integrated within the new system varied and was subject to local arrangement. It's clear from Domesday that Grimkell continued to hold land, but he could have found himself now with a Norman lord as well as Peverel as his overlord.

The Peverel overlordship lasted less than a century. When Henry 1 died in 1135 the English succession was disputed and there was civil war. The fifth (and last) William Peverel found himself supporting the losing side, and when Henry 11 ascended to the throne in 1154 the Peverel estates were confiscated. Although the family was effectively now finished as a major landowner, the barony itself continued under the name of "The Honour of Peverel". So old Peverel lands came back into the gift of the crown after Henry's accession, and it was from then on that a number of important new landowners, or rather chief tenants, came into existence as estates were granted out again. Henry's son, King John, who reigned from 1199-1216, was a particularly important distributor of this largesse.

2 Cantelupe and Chaworth.

It's clear that from the earliest times Watnall evolved as two distinct parcels of land, whose origins might well be found in the two original, and fairly small, pre conquest manors. There is no direct evidence for this, but however they arose and developed, the two parcels formed the basis of the long-lasting distinction between Watnall Chaworth and Watnall Cantelupe. The history of these parcels is both fascinating and complex and will be examined in some detail.

The first parcel, the larger of the two, occupied the greater part of **Watnall Cantelupe** and (eventually) a slice of Chaworth too. The earliest piece of solid evidence appears to be an inquisition of John's time (about 1212) quoted in Thoroton, in which Ralph de Gresley was certified to hold three knight's fees of the Honour of Peverel, one of which was in Greasley {see diagram pg 9}. A knight's fee was simply a parcel of land large enough to support a knight, and like most medieval measures it varied considerably. It's clear from later developments that this Greasley fee included the substantial parcel of land which later devolved to the de Cantelupe family, Lords of Ilkeston, and formed the basis of what became Watnall Cantelupe.

Ralph de Gresley is an early and rather enigmatic figure. The inquisition notes him as holding three knight's fees of the Honour of Peverel, one at Greasley and two at Claindon in Buckinghamshire. Thoroton uses this information to associate him with Hugh, son of Richard, who gifted land at Claindon to Lenton Priory. These relationships would take the family back to the years just after the Conquest, but when their association with Greasley (and Watnall) began is not clear.

From Ralph de Gresley onwards, more substantial evidence starts to appear. During King John's time, Ralph married Isabella Muskham, heiress to the Muskham estates, including Ilkeston locally. Thus the Greasley and Ilkeston estates were united for a time. Ralph and Isabella had a daughter, Agnes, who married Hugh Fitz Ralph, and the various estates then became part of the inheritance of that family. Agnes and Hugh had a son, Ralph, and he had a daughter, Eustacia, who became

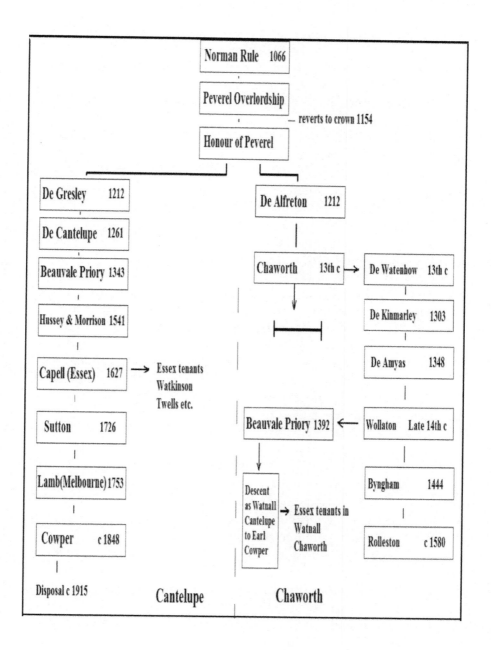

Norman Rule 1066	
Peverel Overlordship	— reverts to crown 1154
Honour of Peverel	

De Gresley 1212

De Cantelupe 1261

Beauvale Priory 1343

Hussey & Morrison 1541

Capell (Essex) 1627 → Essex tenants Watkinson Twells etc.

Sutton 1726

Lamb (Melbourne) 1753

Cowper c 1848

Disposal c 1915

Cantelupe

De Alfreton 1212

Chaworth 13th c → **De Watenhow** 13th c

De Kinmarley 1303

De Amyas 1348

Beauvale Priory 1392 ← **Wollaton** Late 14th c

Descent as Watnall Cantelupe to Earl Cowper → Essex tenants in Watnall Chaworth

Byngham 1444

Rolleston c 1580

Chaworth

his heiress. Eustacia is a pivotal figure in these events as it is she who brought Ilkeston, Greasley and the parcel in Watnall to the highly significant family of de Cantelupe, Lords of Ilkeston.

9

The de Cantelupes had risen to prominence some years previously. William, the first Baron Cantelupe, was prominent in the early part of the 13th century. He held the office of Seneschal, or Steward of the Household, under King John, and was Sheriff of Warwick, Leicester, Worcester and Hereford during part of the reign. He is mentioned as one of John's "evil counsellors" and was in continued attendance at John's side. He was a stalwart during the war against the barons and went on to support the young King Henry on John's death. He was also one of those who signed the confirmation of Magna Carta in 1236.

William, the second Baron Cantelupe, also continued high in the esteem of his king (Henry 111), being appointed Guardian of the Kingdom during the King's absence of 1242. This particular William is important in the Watnall story in that he secured advantageous marriages for his numerous sons. The fourth son, Nicholas de Cantelupe, was married to Eustacia, mentioned above, heiress of Greasley, Ilkeston et al. Nicholas thus became Lord of Ilkeston and simultaneously acquired Greasley, together with the parcel in Watnall.

Nicholas and Eustacia had a son, William, who was born at Lenton Priory in 1262. William took livery of his father's lands in 1283 and married firstly Maud and secondly Eve. By Eve he had two sons, and in the usual medieval effort to confuse posterity called them William and Nicholas.

These two are interesting. William de Cantelupe, the older of the two brothers, was born in 1293, and took livery of his father's lands in 1314, but in 1320 he obtained license to enfeoff (convey to) his brother, the manors of Middle Claydon and Greasley. In any case, William died without issue and his brother Nicholas (d 1355) became his heir, so Nicholas would have acquired the estates anyway.

This particular Nicholas de Cantelupe, from a local point of view, is the most important of all the Cantelupe lords. He became prominent nationally, taking part in Edward 111's continuing wars against Scotland and was made Governor of Berwick upon Tweed. He also served Edward as an ambassador and fought at the Battle of Cressy. He was highly regarded by the King and was granted a "licence to crenellate" his seat at Gresley. This probably resulted in a fortified manor house rather than a true castle, but the King's permission would have been highly prized as a status symbol – all that remains of it now are sundry earthworks next to Greasley Church.

Nicholas also had a profound and lasting impact on the landscape when he founded Beauvale Priory in 1343. The Priory was hugely important locally and its remains can still be seen about a mile from the Horse and Groom Inn at Moorgreen. Its estates were gifted by wealthy landowners, many of whom considered the endowment of religious houses a Godly and righteous duty, especially if they had any aspirations towards eternal life. Nicholas himself, being founder, contributed greatly, and his gift in 1347 included his lands at Watnall, together with "a great company of his villeins, together with the messuages (houses) and bovats of land which they held, with their cattle, suits and sequels".

So the "de Cantelupe" parcel of land in Watnall came to be part of the property of Beauvale Priory, and remained so for 200 years. After that it had an equally complex history which will be briefly summarised.

In the 16th century, Henry V111 quarrelled with the Pope over a plan to divest himself of the first of a number of troublesome wives. He declared himself supreme head of the English Church and dissolved huge numbers of religious houses, including the one at Beauvale. The Priory's lands were confiscated, thus coming into the King's hands where they remained for some years.

After that they were granted out again, firstly to Sir William Hussey in 1541, but re-granted a few years later to Sir Richard Morrison.

In 1627, Elizabeth, daughter and heir of the Morrison family, married Arthur, Baron Capell of Hadham. Arthur fought valiantly in the Civil War on the Royalist side and was beheaded for his troubles in 1649. His son, also named Arthur, succeeded to his father's titles in that year and in 1661 was created Earl of Essex, a position which had previously fallen vacant. So, in 1661, the new Earls of Essex were in possession of Nottinghamshire estates, including those in Watnall, previously owned by the Morrison family and, before that, by Beauvale Priory.

In 1726, it was all change again. The estates were bought by Robert Sutton, head of a very important dynasty which owned large, landed interests in the east of the county, and in 1753 they were sold on again, this time to Sir Matthew Lamb.

Sir Matthew is a fascinating character. He was a Southwell solicitor and acted for some of the most substantial families in Nottinghamshire. He used his position to gather considerable wealth and influence for himself, and in 1740 he married Charlotte Coke of Melbourne Hall, having been her father's confidential adviser. By her, he acquired the Coke estate at Melbourne. Sir Matthew was a hive of industry and wealth-generating acquisition; he actually established the family seat at Brocket Hall in Hertfordshire, another of his purchases.

Although Mathew was the wealth gatherer, the family reached its greatest celebrity with his grandson, William Lamb, the second Viscount Melbourne, who was prime minister from 1834-41. Lamb had a celebrated and disastrous marriage to Lady Caroline Ponsonby, and she herself became notorious as a result of an equally celebrated and disastrous affair with Lord Byron. Lamb was Prime Minister during the early reign of Queen Victoria and was actually responsible for the introduction of the teen-age Queen into the devious and intricate ways of politics.

So, to summarise. A parcel of land in Watnall, originally owned by Nicholas de Cantelupe and given to Beauvale Priory, had, after the dissolution, passed by a chain of purchase or inheritance to become the property of the Lords Melbourne.

On the death of William Lamb, the Melbourne estates passed to his sister, Emily Lamb, and thus to the Cowper family via her marriage to the 5th Earl Cowper in 1805. Emily, Countess Cowper, was an interesting and heady Whig lady in her own right. She enjoyed considerable variation in her romantic life, and later became Lady Palmerston – by marrying her long-time admirer, Lord Palmerston, in 1839.

In 1869, the estates were inherited by her grandson, the 7th Earl Cowper, and it was he who commissioned William Godkin to design his "country cottage" (Beauvale House), built in High Park Wood. Following the 7th Earl's death in 1905 the Nottinghamshire property was left in trust for his widow, Catherine, but on her death in 1913 the estates were broken up and sold from around 1915.

But there was a **second** parcel of land in Watnall: the parcel which was eventually to become **Watnall Chaworth**.

The first piece of really solid evidence about this appears to be an inquisition of John's time (about 1212) quoted in Thoroton, in which William de Alfreton was certified to hold three knight's fees of the Honour of Peverel. Of this, half a fee was in Watnall, but how it came into the possession of the Lords of Alfreton in the first place doesn't appear to be known. What is known with certainty is that the parcel passed, early in the 13th century, to the family of Chaworth, from whence it got its name "Watnall Chaworth".

The family of de Chaurcis originally came from Chaources (now Sourches) near Le Mans in France, and their name later became anglicised to Chaworth. They were to establish a formidable presence in Nottinghamshire. In the middle of the 12th century, Robert de Chaurcis obtained by marriage the manor of Marnham on the Trent, and as the family consolidated, they acquired substantial estates and become major landowners. Their principal seat was established at Wiverton in the 15th century.

As far as Watnall is concerned, an event early in the 13th century is significant. William de Chaurcis, grandson of Robert above, married Alice, daughter and co-heir of Robert de Alfreton, thus bringing Alfreton and the small parcel in Watnall to the Chaworth family.

The Chaworths continue to be mentioned in connection with Watnall for a considerable time after these events, but the records take a significantly different form, of which the following, from "Feudal Aids", is typical. "In 1284, Robert de Watnall (de Watenow) holds in Greasley and its members half a knight's fee of the Escheat of Peverel from Thomas de Chaworth".

So by this time another family had become associated with the parcel - the de Watenows; other evidence suggests that this was actually from some time in the early part of the 13th century. The "Escheat of Peverel" was land originally confiscated by the King from the Peverels for treason, so the Chaworths were holding, in effect, directly from the King. This was known as holding "in chief", and the Chaworths were of a very high class. This was the "baronial" layer - vastly influential landowners whose members were second in rank only to the King himself. The de Watenhows were of lower rank, holding as tenants of the Chaworths. The distinction is important as the recorded history of the Chaworth parcel now appears to follow firmly the line after de Watenhow. The Chaworths are mentioned progressively less in connection with it until, ultimately, it's clear that they have only a notional stake at best. Ultimately, they cease to be mentioned at all; their interest as overlords appears to have become extinguished.

By 1303, after de Watenhow, at least some of the land in Chaworth appears, to have come to Robert de Kinmarley. The de Kinmarleys were substantial tenants of lands outside Watnall, particularly in Kimberley itself where their holding eventually passed to Beauvale Priory. Watnowe is mentioned in a survey of 1316 (the Nomina Villarum) and by then its "Lord" was Robert de Kimberley, although the de Watenhows appeared to retain an interest for some time.

By 1327, at least some land in Watnall had come into the possession of the family of de Amyas. In the subsidy assessment of that year, William de Amyas was rated at 40s 0d for his Nottingham possessions and 7s 0d for those in Watnall. There is a rather confusing document from 1348 in the Borough records, in which William de Amyas and Margery his wife are granted the manors of "Watenowe Chaworth and Ryddynges near Alferton" for life. This is obviously somewhat later than 1327 and to what extent this formalised an existing situation on the ground, or added to it, isn't clear.

William de Amyas, or de Mexborough as he was also known, was one of Nottingham's leading merchants and a mayor four times. He was an incomer to the town, probably related to the Amyas family of York. He had already made his fortune by 1327 when he was Nottingham's second citizen and probably one of the wealthier merchants in England. His name appears frequently in the records of the Borough of Nottingham, but it disappears as quickly as it arises, and he is probably best remembered as the founder of the Amyas chantry in St Mary's Church (Lace Market). He was a ship owner, corn and wool dealer and, later, rural banker and money lender. He began to purchase tenements in Nottingham soon after his arrival in the town, and his town properties became very extensive. His only surviving son, John, was murdered in Nottingham in 1343. He left no will, but his chief beneficiary was his daughter, Joan, who had married Hugh de Spicer, another Nottingham Burgess.

After William de Amyas, the Watnall parcel descended to the family of Wolaton, also of the Borough of Nottingham. The estate came to that family when William de Amyas's younger daughter, Agnes, married Ralph de Wolaton. The Chaworth parcel was in the hands of the Wolatons by 1369, and in 1370 Agnes's son, John de Wolaton, lived in "Watnowe" and his wife's name was Margery. A will of John de Wollaton in the Borough records, dated at Watenhow in May 1382, orders his body to be buried in the Church of Greasley "before the Altar of St James" It also mentions William as being his son and heir.

A very interesting inquisition of 1392 tells us that William Wollaton, presumably son of John above, still held his land in Watnall "of William

Chaworth, by fealty for all service". So we still have the clearly defined medieval pecking order involving the Chaworths at work, with land being parcelled and held by progressively less great men, in return basically for loyalty. The same record also notes the passage of land held by William Wollaton in Watnall Chaworth to Beauvale Priory, which is interesting in that this could be the point at which Chaworth itself began to split into two separate holdings. The smaller part, given to the Priory, followed the same path as Watnall Cantelupe and passed into the hands of Lord Melbourne. The rest of Chaworth descended to the Rollestons.

In 1441, a quitclaim is recorded in the Close Rolls. It says that, in 1440, John Wolaton passed all his rights in the Manor of Watnall Chaworth to a group of about a dozen very high-ranking members of the landed gentry, including John Viscount Beaumont, John la Zouch and William Babyngton. The group also included, very significantly, Richard Byngham, his wife Ellen and their son Richard. The John Wolaton involved here appears to have been the brother of William above and grandson of Ralph and Agnes. The purpose of the quitclaim is not entirely clear, but it appears to be part of a general disposal of much of John's property. The members of the group appear to have been acting as temporary trustees, and a short time later, in 1444, Richard Byngham is described in an inquisition as being "of Watenowe" and was now apparently the outright owner.

This particular Richard Bingham (there were a confusing number of others) was the first to be associated with Watnall, and is of significant interest.

A faded plaque, written in Latin, beneath a window in the chancel at Greasley Church, translates as - "Here lies Helena, wife of Richard Bingham, Knight, formerly a Justice of the King's Bench, who died on the 12th day of February 1448".

So here we have an Ellen, or Helena, who died in 1448 and is buried at Greasley. She married Richard Bingham, and he was, significantly, a Justice of the King's Bench. It would seem to be highly probable that this is the same Richard Byngham, mentioned in the Close Rolls above, who had a wife called Ellen and a son called Richard.

The early life of Richard Bingham the Judge is interesting but shrouded in mystery. He was one of the Carcolston Binghams, but exactly where he fits in with their pedigree is unclear. Thoroton concludes that "Raph (son of Thomas de Bingham of Carcolston) had two brothers, both named John, wherof one might possibly be the father of Sir Richard Bingham the Judge", and that seems to be about as much as is known.

Justice Bingham was appointed to high office on King's Bench in about 1445, and in 1461 he was one of a small group of four, very high-ranking judges, including the Chief Justice. The number of judges on King's Bench was never many more than this so they can be clearly identified; there was never more than one Richard Bingham. Justice Bingham served through the turbulent reigns of Henry V1 and Edward IV at the height of the Wars of the Roses. Henry V1 was murdered at the Tower of London, probably with the approval of his successor; so for Richard to have served one king and then enjoyed seamless re-appointed by the other must say a good deal for his political abilities, if not for his judicial ones. Judge Bingham apparently retired voluntarily from the office sometime before 1471.

It is widely recorded that he married Margaret, the daughter of Sir Baldwin Frevill of Middleton in Warwickshire, and widow of Sir Hugh Willoughby of Wollaton. This appears to have been in about 1448, presumably after the death of his first wife, Helena. He went to live with Margaret at her manor of Middleton, actually at Middleton Hall near Tamworth, and died there in 1476. There is a monument to him in the Church of St John the Baptist at Middleton, wearing his judicial robes. His son, Richard, confusingly married another Margaret, daughter of Sir Thomas Rempston.

The history of Watnall Chaworth after Judge Bingham is again shrouded in considerable mystery. It seems probable that the manor did not pass via his son Richard mentioned above. Judge Bingham appears to have had another son, John, probably by his wife Helena. A fascinating document from 1446 exists in the York registry, in which a license was granted "for John, son of Richard Bingham, to be married to Elizabeth, daughter of Norman Charnells Esq. in an oratory within the manor house of the said Richard at Watnow Chaworth". Not only was John married in the manor house but in 1483 he appears to have died not far away. There is a license from that year in the same group of documents for Elizabeth, widow of John Bingham of Wadnall, "to receive the veil from any Bishop or Abbat". Another intriguing aspect is the early mention of a "manor house," quite possibly the building which pre-dated Watnall Hall.

Early in the 16th century, Richard Bingham of Watnow Chaworth, either grandson or, more probably, great grandson of Judge Bingham, married Anne, one of the four sisters and heirs of Sir Nicholas Strelley of Linby. Their second daughter, Margaret, married Ralph Rolleston, second son of James Rolleston of the Lea, co Derby, bringing Chaworth to the Rollestons. The estate was certainly in their hands by 1580 when there is a record of them being involved in enclosure activity.

The Rollestons added considerably to their lands in 1915, when the Rolleston Trustees bought 533 acres in Greasley and Watnall from the Desborough Trustees after the breakup of the Cowper estates.

3 Early Agricultural Life.

Before industrialisation, England was ruled largely by landed gentry. Beneath them in the pecking order were various groupings of people who actually worked the land: the more important tenant farmers, followed by smaller tenants and then everyone else. An estate survey of 1653 throws some interesting light on the early agricultural set-up as it would have related to ordinary people. It was commissioned by the Hon Dame Elizabeth Capell (Earls of Essex, see above) and lists tenants of the Essex estates with their holdings at that time.

In Watnall Chaworth, eight tenants are listed: William Butler, William Everingham, John Greensmith, Richard Stray, Richard Shaw, Lancelot Shaw, Thomas Wain and Edward Lacey. The largest holding is that of William Butler, at over 70 acres, and the rest are generally between 20 and 40 acres. Interestingly, unlike Watnall Cantelupe, none of these seem to include land in common fields, which indicates that a good part of Chaworth was enclosed by this time. Note that these are the Essex tenants in Chaworth. The other landowner here was Richard Bingham in the 15th century, followed by the Rollestons. Richard Bingham was involved in small scale enclosures by about 1496, and the practice was certainly followed by the Rollestons.

In Watnall Cantelupe there were twelve holdings: James Watkinson, Widow Twells, William Hickton, John Richards, William Watkinson, Thomas Shaw, Lancelot Ellis, Thomas Roberts, Mathew Breedon, Ralph Cheetham, William Harvey and John Severn. The first six of these had holdings of approximately 40 acres, the rest less.

A fascinating aspect of the 1653 survey, as far as Watnall Cantelupe is concerned, is that it gives considerable evidence of an intact open field system. Taking Widow Twells's property as an example, the survey starts by listing her holdings which were not in the "common field": that is enclosed land - "a house with a barn, orchard and croft", together with various other enclosed crofts and closes, totalling about 14 acres. These she will have farmed independently of the communal field system, possibly by employing poorer "landless" people from the village. The survey then goes on to list her properties (lands) in "the common field".

A typical entry would be "Holy Well Furlong, one land bounded with James Watkinson west and Lancelot Ellis east." There were three common fields in Cantelupe in 1653 – Middle Field, Bird Stubing Field, and Row Oak Field - and compared to modern fields they were vast.

A "land" was the basic agricultural unit. It was simply a convenient size for the operation of a plough team, nominally 22 yards wide, but often narrower depending on the terrain, and nominally 220 yards long, although this too varied considerably. The plough team laboured up and down the land, starting in the middle and working towards the outside edge. This produced a characteristic ridge in the middle and a furrow at each edge. One or more lands were grouped together into "strips", which formed a nominal day's work for a plough team, and the strips were grouped together into "furlongs" or "flats" as they were more commonly known locally. Furlongs were groups of strips arranged conveniently within the common field, mainly with a view to drainage and access.

The 1653 records are difficult to interpret, but a close study of field names can yield some tentative conclusions as to what this all might have looked like on the ground. These are set out on the map {pg 51}. Note that this shows features which actually existed at different times: the mid 17th century field system for example, and the 19th century rail network. It also shows some later modifications to the road system. The original lane through the village appears to have followed approximately the line of Holly Road and Trough Lane. Scattered along the principal lane would have been the hamlet's farms, surrounded by their "private" closes. Almost everyone lived in a village in early times, isolated homesteads, such as the much later "Common Farm", were a rarity. Remains of some of the original buildings are still there; the Hollies for example has recently been dated to about 1450.

Surrounding the hamlet were its open fields. To the south of Cantelupe was Row Oak Field, bordering on to Kimberley's field system. On the east side of the Nottingham Road were Middle Field and Bird Stubbin Field. An unusual feature of Bird Stubbin Field, gleaned from 19th century field names, is that it appears to have been divided into two parts by the common. Nonetheless, it will almost certainly have been worked by the manor court as a single agricultural unit. Close in near the village, another name appears amongst the closes and furlongs, "Holywell", reflecting the name of a significant local water system. The Holy Well Spring rose on the southwestern boundary of Watnall

19

Chaworth and flowed southwards as a surface stream, past the current site of Kimberley Brewery, before turning west and eventually joining the Gilt Brook. It was exploited by both Kimberley breweries and progressively culverted as the Industrial Revolution progressed. Nowadays it doesn't finally see the light of day until it reaches a point close to the Hogs Head Inn.

There is some solid evidence from 1724 of two areas of common in Watnall Cantelupe. An estate survey by George Capps lists "The Common Cliffe" where there was "comon pasture belonging to all the farms except John and William Watkinson". Some of the farms had "sumer gates" and some "winter gates". The Cliff still towers over the old village of Cantelupe and a gate in this context was a right to pasture animals. The other common listed by Capps amounted to 95 acres and "entirely belongs to Sir Robert Sutton's tenants, no others having any privilege therin" (Sutton owned what later became Lord Melbourne's estate).

Other aspects of the agricultural system are also worth mentioning. In a common field system, all the tenants (and freeholders) had to co-operate in a common agricultural programme. A higher authority, the manor court, was required both to determine what the programme would be and to enforce discipline; the court's officers would, for example, make sure that everyone had removed his crops in time for stubble to be used for grazing in the autumn. The 1653 survey mentions a "Court Leete and Barron kept in ye Mannr at Michms". The "Mannr" was "Bevall", but this was also the Lord's court with ultimate authority for agricultural discipline amongst Essex tenants in Watnall. Substantial responsibility was delegated to a "jury" of local people, who were appointed at periodic meetings of the court. The jury had to deal with any persons felt to be contravening local bylaws and exercised its authority via a number of court officials - the pinder for example was responsible for stray animals, and a pinfold was recorded until relatively recently, opposite the Royal Oak inn. A fairly intact set of court documents exists from a meeting of Beauvale Manor Court in 1753. In this case, a jury of 14 men was sworn in by the Lord's steward in October. A "suit roll" (list of tenants under the court's jurisdiction) is recorded, and it then goes on to itemise the decisions made by the court, which seem quaint now but were the stuff of life in England in 1753: hedges to be made, Dorothy Watkinson to destroy her ducks and drake, all persons owning pigs and horses to take them off the common, and

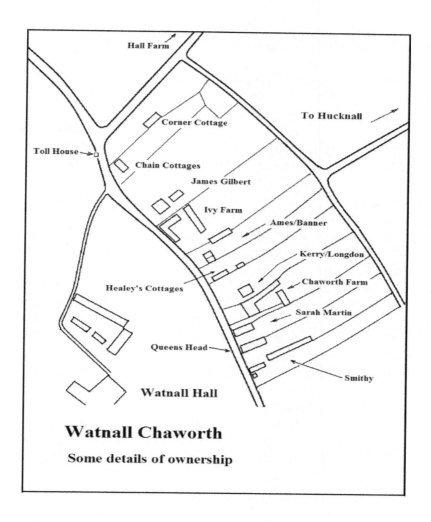

Watnall Chaworth

Some details of ownership

so on. There is also documentary evidence of a similar court operating in Watnall Chaworth, although no actual court records appear to have survived.

By the mid-19th century, Watnall had been enclosed, and comprised quite a large number of isolated farmsteads such as Brooksbreasting and Crowhill, associated now with the more modern pattern of concentrated private holdings. A number of other farms, however, remained within the village, strung out north to south along the main thoroughfare, reflecting the older pattern of communal cultivation. In the hamlet of Chaworth, the map looked rather like a piano keyboard, with Rolleston tenants living cheek by jowl with those of Lord Melbourne. In Cantelupe, the pattern was a little different as it only had one owner (Lord Melbourne). It's illuminating to look at individual holdings within the two hamlets, together with their tenants, in a little more detail.

Starting at the north end of **Chaworth**, the present **Hall Farm** was built in the late 19th century. After that it became home to the Shaw Clay family. Both the Shaws and Clays are well known locally, and when they intermarried, they often used both names. In this case, Joseph Shaw Clay was the tenant at Hall farm. He was there, together with his wife Kezia, for many years in the early 20th c.

Fronting on to Narrow Lane was a small farm, seemingly known later as **Watnall Corner Cottage**. In 1841, this appears to have been a sizeable holding of about 40 acres, owned by Lancelot Rolleston and tenanted by Stephen Watson. By 1853, Watson was occupying Holly Bush Farm, together with his old holding at the corner. Presumably this is the time at which the building ceased to be a farm as such. In 1910 it was occupied by William Brown. John Hobbs, later a well-known Kimberley teacher, moved in with his new wife, Florence, after their marriage in 1914. Their son John, also a well-known local musician, recalls that at the time of his residence the building was split into two cottages, the other people being called Griffiths. Members of the Banner family are also recorded here.

Heading south again, fronting on to Main Road, was a group of three dwellings known as **Chain Cottages**, associated with a toll bar in the form of a chain across the road, of which more elsewhere. Mr Hobbs (Junior) recalls that they were burnt down in about 1897 and rebuilt. They were occupied in 1910 by John Webb, Joseph Smith and Arthur Woodcock; originally part of the Melbourne estate, they were sold to Lancelot Rolleston in 1915 following the death of Earl Cowper.

Heading south again along Main Road we come to a smallholding of about 10 acres, owned by Viscount Melbourne and occupied, in 1853, by **James Gilbert**. By 1910 it had passed to Melbourne's successor in the estates, Earl Cowper, and occupied by Elizabeth Millership. Alfred Millership bought the freehold from Earl Cowper's trustees in 1914.

Next to the Millership smallholding on Main Road was **Ivy House Farm**. In 1853 this was owned by Lancelot Rolleston and occupied by William Twells, who seems to have inherited about 80 acres from his mother Frances. By 1861, Matthew Twells seems to have been the tenant and his family remained at the farm for about 20 years. By 1881, John Farnsworth was in occupation with his wife and family, including a son, Fred, aged 3, and by 1891 the family had expanded to encompass 4 daughters and 6 sons, including Fred, now 13, and his younger brothers Frank and Sidney. By the early 1930s Frank was farming at Ivy House and Sidney was at the Hollies. Ivy Farm is also unusual in that it seems to have had an early beer house associated with it – the Wheatsheaf, recorded in Whites Directory of 1832. Next to Ivy Farm were two cottages, together with small gardens, occupied in 1853 by Elizabeth Ames and Thomas Banner.

John Banner had a small farm of about 40 acres in Chaworth, described in Melbourne estate records from 1824. In 1841 he is recorded there with his wife Sarah, and also William and Sarah Banner, presumably his son and daughter in law. These two reappear, farming in Watnall Cantelupe in 1851, see later. Unfortunately, for reasons which aren't clear, John Banner's farm does not appear on the 1853 Shaw map; the nearest match appears to be the farm occupied by John Bonser. This was occupied in 1910 by Joseph Healey and sold to Lancelot Rolleston in 1915. John Banner resumed a presence in Chaworth for several more years, but it seems clear that the centre of gravity of the family's farming operation had now moved to Cantelupe.

Next to Healey's cottage, in 1853, were small cottages occupied by William Kerry and John Longdon, and then we come to **Chaworth Farm**, which no longer exists but was to the north of the present Queen's Head. Rolleston family deeds pin down the site to 1755, when it was owned by John Everingham of Bilborow, gent, and occupied by Robert Clark. The deeds include the farm and surrounding land, which encompass the present site of the Queen's Head Inn, as well as a smithy, which was in premises immediately to the south. Other papers, originally lodged at Melbourne Hall, mention a William Everingham farming in Watnall Chaworth in 1653. He then occupied about 20 acres and was a tenant of the Earls of Essex, whose lands ultimately came into the ownership of, firstly, Lord Melbourne and, later, Earl Cowper. At some stage, shortly after 1653, the Everingham family must have become freeholders as they do not appear in tenants lists for either the Melbourne or Rolleston estates after the beginning of the 18th century.

Towards the end of the 18th century the Chaworth Farm site was progressively broken up and sold off by the heirs of the Everingham family. By 1853, Lord Melbourne had acquired the farm itself, the tenant

23

being John Shaw, now farming 114 acres. Melbourne also acquired the smithy which lay to the south of the Queen's Head. By 1853, Lancelot Rolleston owned premises which existed between the farm and the Queens Head, which were tenanted in 1853 by Sarah Martin. The Queen's Head itself followed a different course, discussed elsewhere. In 1915, Lancelot Rolleston rounded off his estates in the area when he obtained a large portfolio of property following the breakup of the Cowper estates. Both the smithy and Chaworth Farm were included in this purchase. The Shaw family were tenants at Chaworth Farm for many years from about the mid-19th century, making their last appearance in documents from the 1890s. After that Arthur Woodcock became the tenant.

Moving south again into **Watnall Cantelupe,** to the corner of Trough Road and Main Road, and the ancient farm known as **"The Hollies"** {see map pg 25}. It has an obvious timber frame which has been dated using tree ring technology to around 1452–5, so it should appear in some guise or other in all later surviving records. Its appearance in the 1841 Tithe Award is fairly straightforward. The award contains a numbered map, and the Hollies is parcel no 32. All the land in Cantelupe was owned by Lord Melbourne in 1841, and the Hollies, together with its associated holding (about 73 acres), was tenanted by Henry Sleight. Sleight also appears in an interesting earlier record from 1824 in which the buildings are described in some detail: "A dwelling house containing a parlour, kitchen, wash house, two chambers and a lumber room, two barns of five bays and a threshing place, two stables for five horses, cowhouse for four cows, cartshed and hogs court. These buildings are part brick, part stone walls, part thatched part tiled, also a small house in two tenements, brick and thatched". When going back further, things become more problematical. No maps exist and early records weren't designed to be read several centuries later. In 1724, the likeliest tenant for the Hollies would appear to be Daniel Watkinson, and earlier still, in 1653, possibly James Watkinson, although these last two are very speculative.

By 1853 Henry Sleight, now an esquire, had left the Hollies and is listed as occupying "Newthorpe Cottage, garden and pleasure ground". By this time, Francis Read Grammar was at the Hollies with his small daughters Gertrude and Lucy. The Grammars were important farmers in the area, having large holdings in Newthorpe as well as Watnall. By

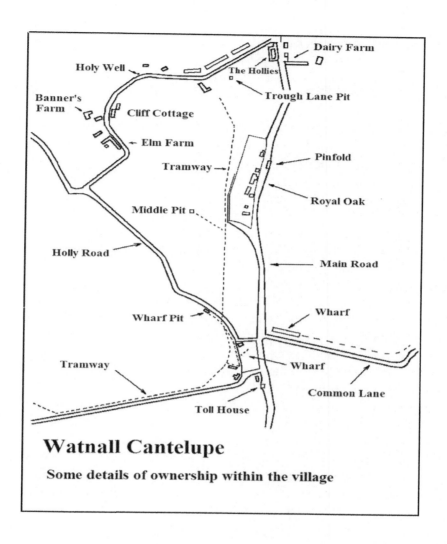

Watnall Cantelupe

Some details of ownership within the village

1853, Francis Grammar's holding at the Hollies, at 123 acres, was much larger than Henry Sleight's in 1841. A process of logical, but piecemeal, consolidation was absorbing smaller holdings into the bigger farms. Francis Grammar appears to have stayed at the Hollies into the early 1860s. After this the farm had a succession of tenants. By 1885, Mrs Sarah Allcock is being listed in trade directories as farming at the Hollies, followed in about 1900 by Mr Robert Holbrook from Wilford. By 1910, William Buchanan was in occupation, and five years later the farm was conveyed in its entirety to Lancelot Rolleston as part of his parcel of acquisitions in Watnall, following the breakup of the old Cowper estates. The Buchanan family remained as tenants until the early 1930s when Sidney Farnsworth, latterly of Ivy Farm, took over. Mr Cooper, in 1976, could remember Sid Farnsworth at the Hollies, still hale and hearty at the age of 89.

Immediately opposite the Hollies was **"Dairy House Farm"**. In 1976, Mr Cooper noted that it had been pulled down with only one barn left standing. The site appears to have spent a good deal of its history in multiple occupation. In 1841, three tenants of Lord Melbourne are recorded, farming about 180 acres between them: Charles Birks, William Clarke and David Towle. The same families appear in records from 1824, and the name Towle goes back even further, with Jonathan Towle recorded as a substantial farmer at Watnall in 1724.

By 1853, only Elizabeth and William Clarke, mother and son, remained of the original Dairy House tenants, with 46 acres; the others were new, small cottagers, including Joseph Fox and Ann Bainbridge, a schoolmistress, with only small amounts of land. By 1853, intense consolidation was taking place. Three major farming tenants had emerged in Cantelupe by this time: Robert Watkinson at Elms Farm with about 100 acres, Francis Grammar at the Hollies with about 123 acres, and William Banner on Trough Lane with about 156 acres. These larger holdings had absorbed land from a number of smaller tenancies, including those at the Dairy House, which existed in 1841. The Clarke family appears to have remained at Dairy House for many years, with a William Clarke, farmer, being recorded in the 1890s. By 1901, William Jackson, a wheelwright, and his wife Kate are living on the site with their family and, shortly afterwards, John Henry Robinson is recorded. The Jacksons had a smallholding and Robinson was farming about 30 acres. Both these holdings were acquired by Lancelot Rolleston in 1915. By 1932, Miss Agnes Buchanan is recorded at the site, and she was dairy farming in 1941.

Moving south again along Trough Lane, a well-known feature is Holy Well. According to local folklore a small boy had a miraculous recovery here after being baptised by a priest. Further along is **Cliff Cottage**, which was a sizeable farm of about 50 acres at the time of the 1841 tithe award, owned by Lord Melbourne and occupied by Joseph Walton. Walton is also recorded there in records from 1824. By 1853, John Clarke Junior occupied the site. He was a wheelwright and farmer. His holding was about 10 acres, so by now it had been much reduced and

26

absorbed into other farms. The Clarke family remained at the holding for many years; in 1910, Mary Ann Clark still occupied 10 acres, which was purchased by Lancelot Rolleston in 1915. Mrs Mary Ann Clarke is recorded as a cow keeper in directories from 1941.

Opposite to Cliff Cottage, almost at the entrance to the modern Oxbury Road, was another important farm, now gone. It was occupied, together with about 74 acres in 1841 by William Watkinson. The family has been noted before, farming in the area since at least 1650. In 1841, William Watkinson was being assisted by his nephew, **William Banner**, aged 25, and wife Phoebe. These two were destined to become very prosperous farmers. By 1853, as noted previously, great consolidation was taking place. William Banner and his wife were by now running the farm, which had expanded to about 156 acres, and William Watkinson, by now retired, appears to have continued living with them. The couple had a daughter, Mary Ann, who, it seems, was destined for even greater prosperity. She married Robert Goodall Hanson, the Kimberley brewer in 1865, and they had a large family of eleven children. For a short period, they were resident at Watnall Hall before moving to their new family home at Cloverlands, Kimberley. William Banner had retired by 1881 and the farm was split up sometime before 1914. In that year it was sold by Earl Cowper's trustees, and the farm buildings on Trough Lane, together with about 13 acres of closes, were bought by **Thomas Coleman**. The majority of the lands associated with William Banner's old farm, however, were purchased by Lancelot Rolleston, and formed the holdings of the relatively recently built Common Farm.

At the corner of Trough Lane and Trough Road was, and still is, **Elms Farm**, another of the ancient residences of the Watkinson family. Robert Watkinson was farming 97 acres here in 1841 with his wife Mary and family, although, as has been noted previously, the Watkinsons are recorded farming locally in documents from as far back as the mid-17th century. Robert Watkinson's son, John, seems to have taken over by 1881 but, by 1910, John Bolton is recorded, farming about 90 acres. "Bolton's Farm" was conveyed to Lancelot Rolleston by Earl Cowper's trustees in 1915, and John Bolton continued to farm here until the mid-1920s when Henry Smalley seems to have taken over.

The busiest part of modern Cantelupe comprises the attractive grouping of cottages along Main Road extending on either side of the **Royal Oak inn**, of which more later. Mr Hadfield, writing in 1985, has pointed out that when the old road from Nottingham was turnpiked in

1758 it was probably straightened. It would originally have run through the hamlet in a loop, following approximately the lines of Trough Lane and Holly Road. The bulk of Cantelupe village, presently strung out along Main Road, grew up along the later line of the turnpike road. Later on still, in the very early part of the 20th century, the old village was by-passed yet again with the construction of Trough Road.

The "newer" part of the village, including the Royal Oak, was home for quite a number of families living in small cottages. It seems to have been arranged on quite a varied plan, but typically the cottages held a small patch of land at the rear, which by 1850 backed on to the tramway running from Trough pit through to the coal wharf. Conditions were probably quite cramped. The building which was later replaced by the late 19th century extension to the Royal Oak, itself appears to have been split into four separate holdings, each with its own small garden. Families living in this part of the village in 1853 included the Smiths, Whitelocks, Burrows, Robinson, Sterland and Twells.

4 The Industrial Revolution: Turnpike Roads; Framework Knitting; Railways.

The Industrial Revolution: Watnall is a curiosity in that it is situated between two important areas of centuries-old industrial activity: Nottingham and the Erewash Valley, yet until quite recently it has remained a largely undisturbed, rural enclave. From about the latter part of the 18th century, the entire area was caught up in a maelstrom of complex and rapidly moving industrial development which became known nationally as the Industrial Revolution. From about the first half of the 19th century, the old landscape of small villages, scattered about in an open, rural landscape of fields, began to change rapidly as other less picturesque activities advanced. In Kimberley, the old pastoral village, described by Throsby in about 1790 as "one of the most romantic I have seen in these parts", with its patchwork fields and apparently unchanging way of life, entered a more ugly, industrial age. But Watnall was not so profoundly affected as other places. There was no large-scale industrialisation, although there were both mines and railways. It retained its rural character, which ironically lead to much greater change in our own lifetimes as people came to regard the area as an attractive place to live.

The Turnpike Roads. By the latter part of the 17th century, the decrepit condition of the roads nationally had become a real problem. A better system was needed, and local committees called "Turnpike Trusts" started to emerge. They were enabled by Act of Parliament to fund road maintenance, by raising tolls at certain bars across the roads. The trusts spread slowly, reaching Nottingham early in the 18th century. The first turnpike locally was set up in 1758 and ran between Chapel Bar, Nottingham, and Newhaven House in Derbyshire. It was known as the Alfreton Turnpike road and passed through Watnall along the line of the modern Main Road. It was set up by public subscription with an initial capital of £7000, its principal shareholders being local gentry, colliery owners, clergy and the more substantial type of farmer. The colliery owners obviously hauled coal along the route, and it appears to have inflicted a good deal of heavy wear and tear. The first general meeting of the trust was at the George Inn, Alfreton, in 1759, where the position of a number of gates was agreed (more followed) and, interestingly, it was also agreed to enforce statutory labour. This was the system which preceded the turnpikes, and involved parishioners being obliged to turn out for a number of days each year to maintain the local roads. The trusts seized on this residual duty as a source of free labour, and its lack of popularity can be imagined. The public disliked having to pay for the new roads in any guise and often went to inordinate lengths to avoid the activity. The relatively small number of surviving trust records are full of incidents of toll avoidance and bad humour. In 1766, for example, a number of tenants at Brackenfield behaved in "a very unbecoming and insolent manner" to the Commissioners. No doubt it arose from their having to pay tolls, and the protest resulted in an effective increase.

The Derby to Mansfield road through Eastwood was turnpiked slightly later than the Alfreton road, in 1764, together with a link through from Eastwood to Nuthall, thus completing the local network. Two toll houses are recorded in Watnall in 1853. One was close to the junction between the current Newdigate Road and Main Road in Cantelupe. The one in Chaworth was at Chain Cottages, close to the junction between Main Road and Narrow Lane. Both had gone by 1880.

The turnpike roads were the first link in an improving local transport system. They were followed in the 18th century by the canals, particularly along the Erewash Valley, and then, of course, the railways.

Framework Knitting, and Lace The stocking frame was an early arrival in the East Midlands. It was invented in 1589 by William Lee of Calverton, allegedly because a prospective lady love was focusing more attention on her knitting than on him. It didn't remain here for long. Lee took it first to London, where he failed to gain much support from the Tudor court, and then to Northern France, where it became the backbone of a flourishing local silk knitting industry. Lee died in France, but the machine returned to London with his brother and began a slow process of acceptance.

The East Midlands became a vitally important producer of hosiery during the second half of the 17th century, when the stocking frame began to return home in considerable numbers. There were a number of reasons for this - the growing power of the trade organisation in

London being one. By 1782, nearly ninety percent of twenty thousand stocking frames in use nationally were in the East Midlands; at this time, it was largely a "cottage" industry. Parish records for the area contain large numbers of entries for people who earned their living in the trade. The Rolleston family also appear to have provided financial support for a number of apprenticeships locally, and records survive from the first half of the 18th century which include a good many indentures for framework knitters.

Railways. The Midland was the first railway to serve Nottingham and its coalfield, and by the middle of the 19th century had acquired a virtual monopoly over South Derbyshire and Nottinghamshire mineral traffic. But by 1850 the Great Northern had reached the city itself from an unlikely direction — the east. It had obtained running rights over an obscure branch from Grantham and was intent on exploiting them to the full. There was no love lost between the two companies to say the least, to the extent that when the Great Northern's first express from London arrived over the new route it was impounded by the Midland and locked up in a shed for several months.

The Great Northern greedily began looking at the potential in the coalfield further west. The company decided to strike straight into the Midland's heartland. It built a line which ran from Colwick, through what is now the northern perimeter of Nottingham, including Watnall, Kimberley and Ilkeston, to Derby. There was also a branch to Pinxton which exploited the lucrative Erewash Valley pits. The strategy worked. The new line first carried traffic in 1875 and became extremely busy.

The Midland was exceedingly rattled, even before the new line opened, and in 1872 decided to react to the Great Northern's proposed incursion into its territory. A rival route was promoted, which linked its Erewash Valley line at Bennerley to the Nottingham-Mansfield line at Basford, via Kimberley and Watnall. It was never a great success. Six passenger trains a day used the route during the early part of the 20th century, but they were withdrawn as a World War 1 economy measure. The line became a goods branch to Kimberley from Basford after 1917, carrying beer, coal and general freight.

Thus, two major railway companies built lines through Watnall, and they were both very problematical. The Great Northern's route involved the construction of a tunnel under the B600 and a deep cutting between Watnall and Kimberley. The slightly later Midland line also made a

31

considerable impact on the local landscape. It too required a tunnel and a very spectacular cutting, which still extends from Kimberley, north east of the present brewery buildings. The Midland also provided station facilities at Watnall, unlike its competitor.

The Great Northern decided to tap into local colliery traffic by building a short, single-line branch, to link with Barber Walker's extensive network of private colliery lines at Watnall Top {see map pg 51}. The private line, as mentioned above, headed northwards from the site of Watnall Old Pit, to link with Watnall New Colliery, and then High Park, Moorgreen, and Barber Walker's other pits in the Eastwood area. Coal was brought to sidings at Watnall using colliery stock and then transferred to the GN. The slightly later Midland graced Watnall with a station, seemingly identical to the one in Kimberley, and a dedicated branch line which ran northwards, parallel with Barber Walker's private railway, into Watnall New Colliery.

5 Mining.

The history of the whole area, from the earliest times, is inextricably linked with mining. There have even been suggestions that a small industry could have been active during the Roman period. The exposed coalfield lies roughly to the west of a line drawn from Nottingham to Chesterfield, and in this area, coal outcrops at the surface. All early mining was carried out here, owing to the limited scope of contemporary technology.

Coal burning first appears in Nottinghamshire's records in 1257 when Queen Eleanor was so offended by smoke that she changed her plans to stay at Nottingham Castle. The earliest surviving copy in Britain of a lease to mine coal is from Notts and is dated 1316 - it concerns a mine in Cossall. Many earlier mines appear to cluster around Wollaton, Strelley, Cossall and Bilborough because of their close proximity to the navigable Trent, but localised mining did take place in the Greasley area, and there are a number of early references from the locality. The monks of Beauvale Priory appear to have been active in the 14th century and, in 1483, a certain Elisha Dey of Watnall Cantelupe was hauling "pitte coals" to Nottingham. The first record of the Rollestons leasing coal rights appears to be in 1636.

From about the middle of the 16th century the demand for coal began to rise rapidly, owing to the increasing scarcity of wood. The industry remained small scale and localized, however, until the momentous transport improvements of the Industrial Revolution: the turnpike roads and canals of the 18th century, and the railways of the 19th century. The early colliers burrowed into seams for short distances or sank small shafts, the coal being extracted from around the shaft bottom forming a "bell pit". Bell pit working was obviously inefficient, and the next stage was to drive headings into the seam from the pit bottom with side galleries known as stalls. This was called post and stall working. There was steady technological advance throughout the 18th century. Horse driven pumps gradually gave way to steam engines for drainage, ventilation improved, and the whim gin was introduced. Transport too was on the march. The Erewash Canal opened from

Trent Lock to Langley Mill in 1779, and the Nottingham Canal, linking Langley Mill with Nottingham and the Trent, opened a little later in 1796.

One of the greatest names in Nottinghamshire mining had very early local roots. **Francis Barber** was born at Selston in 1687, exactly a century before the formation of the famous Barber Walker partnership. What isn't so well known is that for most of that time the family was active in its own right, both as coal masters and in farming. Francis was living at Greasley Castle when he died in the year 1762 and the family appear to have been there since at least 1706, when John Barber of Greasley Castle is recorded seeking liberty of a "coleroad" in Watnall from the Earls of Essex. He was certainly involved in mining at the time, as he leased rights in Selston from the Earls of Essex in 1708. Accounts from "Mr Barber" for coal "got at Kimberley pits" cover the years between 1728 and 1740, and in 1766 a new proposal was on the table "for letting the Duke of Rutland's & Sir Mathew Lamb's collieries in the Parish of Griesley to Mr. Robert Barber". This included coal "that shall be got and sold within the Hamlet of Kimberley" and also "coal got and sold within Griesly Castle Farm being his own property during the term".

The Barbers formed an early partnership with the **Fletchers**, an important mining family who were active principally in the Heanor area, but also operated in Greasley, Kimberley, Strelley and Bilborough. Francis Barber of Greasley Castle married Elizabeth Fletcher, originally of Stainsby Hall, in 1731, thereby cementing a family as well as a business bond. Elizabeth and Francis themselves had a large family of sons and daughters, which formed the Barber element of the better known, and later, **Barber Walker** partnership. Of their children, John Barber was born in 1734, Robert Barber was born at Greasley Castle in 1737, and Thomas Barber was born at Greasley Castle in 1738. The male line of the Fletcher family died out in 1766 and a good part of their property passed to the Barbers via Elizabeth.

By 1800, another potent, but locally brief, force had appeared in the area. James Potter was a farmer and potter of Ilkeston Mill and Greasley. Two of his five sons, James and Samuel, became coal masters. James seems to have lived in Ilkeston, whereas his brother was resident, at least for a time, at Greasley Castle. The partnership of **Potter and Bourne** seems to have started at Ilkeston and, by 1791, James Potter and Gervas Bourne were proposing to sink a mine there. The partnership appears

34

The Royal Oak

Watnall Cantelupe

to have become active in Greasley from about 1800, and their activities are recorded as later additions to maps from 1765 and 1798. These activities are quite extensive. There was a large recovery from the top hard seam under Kimberley by Messrs Potter and Bourne, and "Mr Potter's" name appears associated with numerous pit sites. Potter and Bourne were also very active in the Giltbrook Valley, although in one annotation east of Reckoning House it's noted that in 1806 "they had only two pits and got very little coal, it having been worked many years before" - possibly by the Barbers. The partnership had been wound up by 1824.

One notable relic of the Potter and Bourne era appears to have been "Greasley Engine". This was close to the western bank of the Gilt Brook, near Wood Pit Cottage {see map pg 51}. It was clearly a pumping engine and is referred to in correspondence from 1819, which took place after Potter and Bourne's pits in the area had been "drowned out" (flooded). It was connected to an extensive subterranean drainage level called the "Greasley Level" which extended for miles under Greasley. The buildings associated with the engine appear to have been extended and provided a home for a substantial group of residents, right up to the beginning of the 1900s. At the time of the 1881 census "Greasley Engines" comprised 8 inhabited dwellings, housing 35 people.

Over the years, a complex network of roads and tramways was built in the Giltbrook Valley to carry coal, firstly to the turnpike at Giltbrook, and later to both the Erewash and Nottingham canals. The Barbers were mining for most of the 18th century and highly likely to have been engaged in this activity. Potter and Bourne were also active in the valley from about 1800, when it's recorded that they were about to make a railway from "Greasley Colliery" to the Nottingham Canal. Sanderson's map of 1835 shows that by that date routeways heading south towards Giltbrook had also been extended north towards the Greasley engine and then eastwards, crossing the Gilt Brook towards Watnall Wood.

Some years later, there were further developments. **James Morley** of Nuthall was one of the partners in the ill-fated association of Thomas North, Wakefield and Morley. **Thomas North**, who was also active in the Giltbrook Valley, was nearly always in financial difficulties, and the partnership with Morley broke up in 1849 after much acrimony. In 1852, James Morley took out a lease from Lancelot Rolleston, allowing access to coal reserves at Watnall, and borrowed a large amount of money from, amongst others, I+R Morley the Heanor textile manufacturers. Morley built an extensive mining operation centred on Wood Pit Cottage, which was described in 1853 as a "house, close with workshops & yard amounting to about 5 acres", and an inclined railway was built from there to another site he rented: "Town End Field and Coal Wharf", later occupied by Hall Farm. Another branch was built to a land sale site on the main road, close to its junction with Narrow Lane. Morley worked from old shafts which he refurbished, probably old Barber and Walker workings which originally had their outlet to the Nottingham Canal via the Giltbrook Valley. Morley wasn't lucky. A court case took place in 1858, in which his creditors recovered all his mining and personal assets. He ended up with "the wearing apparel of him the said James Morley" – losing literally everything except the shirt on his back. The colliery apparatus was sold in 1858 and comprised amongst other items: eight steam engines, nine boilers, 150 tram wagons, 43 railway trucks, several miles of rails and a good many buildings, to be demolished within a month, as well as 30,000 bricks.

Up to the early part of the 19th century, mines were still small and worked only the Top Hard seam. In Watnall itself there were a number of pits of this age, working to a depth of about 400 feet. The earliest was near Trough Lane, and it was probably operating as early as the 1820s.

The partnership of the **Barber and Walker** families towered over the mining history of the area, and their company, Barber Walker and Co. Ltd. had widespread and lasting effects upon the landscape, notably in the construction of canals and, later, railways. Evidence from 1842 indicates that there were three pits in Watnall owned by the company at that time: Trough Lane, Middle and Wharf. They were all linked by an interesting system of horse drawn tramways to a landsale wharf, which occupied the site between Holly Road and Newdigate Road {see map pg 25}. Another tramway ran SW from here, along the line of Newdigate Road, to link with yet another pit, which existed on what later became the Cloverlands site. The landsale wharf was obliterated by the Midland Railway, and later in the 19th century a new wharf arose on the other side of Main Road, this time linked in with the local rail system {see map pg 25}.

A report written in 1855 by Robert Harrison, Barber Walker's most famous manager, notes that "a new colliery had been sunk to the top hard seam at Watnall". This was the most important of the earlier group of mines. It was alongside the Watnall – Nuthall road, and is now a tree covered mound in the Larkfield estate. It had a depth of 125 yards and was apparently the seventh shaft sunk to work the Top Hard seam in the vicinity of Watnall village. It seems to have been quite a productive pit as, in 1872, Harrison wrote again that it was "unnecessary to say anything about this colliery beyond that it is in a good working state and is making, as it always has made, in proportion to the capital invested, a good and satisfactory profit." It was linked to other Barber Walker pits in the area by a rather impressive private mineral line, which the company constructed sometime between 1850 and 1860. The line transcribed a huge arc from Langley Mill, around the head of the Giltbrook Valley to Watnall {see map pg 51}. The first locomotive was working by 1854, and the line eventually linked together Watnall, New Watnall, High Park and Moorgreen pits, with branches to Brinsley and Selston. Towards the end of the 19th century, a link was constructed to the new wharf at the end of Common Lane.

After about 1840 the mining industry underwent rapid technological change, with safer, high-capacity shafts, improved ventilation, improved underground haulage systems and, of course, later in the century, the railways. By the 1860s and 70s, Barber Walker was improving and building collieries at a rapid rate. The first of the new pits was High Park, opened in 1861. Moor Green followed in 1872, and in the same year work started on Watnall New Colliery at a depth of over 900 feet. The older pits in Watnall continued into the start of the new era. Old Watnall Colliery itself ceased production in 1879. Watnall New Colliery was sunk through an outcrop of Marl, and a brickworks grew up next to it, with associated chimneys, which still form a very prominent feature of the landscape. The plant was in production from the 1920s and closed in about 1967.

6 Methodism; the Victoria Institute and the WI.

The roots of Methodism lay in a rather austere religious society founded by Charles and John Wesley at Oxford in about 1730. Irreverent undergraduates formulated various nicknames for the group, but the one which stuck was "The Methodists" because of the exceedingly methodical manner in which members organised their spiritual lives. John Wesley towered over the early history of Methodism and travelled the country preaching for fifty years from about 1740.

After his death in 1791 there was serious discontent amongst his followers, largely over the question of how independent, if at all, the Methodists should be of the mother Church of England - Wesley himself had always been an advocate of remaining within the church. Various splinter groups formed. In 1797, the Methodist New Connection broke away. In 1810, another group calling themselves the Primitive Methodists left, and a third separated in 1849 called the United Methodist Free Church. Strangely enough, the hard living folk of the Nottinghamshire coalfield took Methodism in all its denominations to their hearts and were enthusiastic about it in a way they never seemed to be about the established church. The Methodist chapel and its procedures lacked the cold austerity of the parish church. It was a place where mining families could sing rumbustiously, listen to hell-fire oratory and feel at home. The chapel became a true competitor to the public house as a centre of community life. Chapels were actively encouraged by the colliery owners, many of whom were Methodists themselves. They were seen as a sobering and benign influence and were also vitally important in that their Sunday schools provided the first rudimentary education for boys from mining families; it's arguable that this lead ultimately to increasing vision in the mining communities and a desire for progress and change.

Many of the larger local towns had sizeable Methodist communities which featured strongly in the, not always peaceful, in-fighting. In Watnall, as might be expected, things were somewhat quieter. Papers at the Notts Archives record the lease, in 1865, of a piece of land at Watnall from Lord and Lady Palmerston to Messrs Greensmith, Whetton and

Victoria
Institute
1897

others, and sometime later a trust was declared to build a chapel, or meeting house, on this land.

This was the United Methodist Free Church, and it seems to have lasted for around 30 years, a rather short time by local standards, as in about 1895 a period of great change set in. From about that time, the chapel appears to have been known increasingly as "The Institute". Clearly the demand for more diverse activity within the community was growing. The trend gathered momentum and in 1897 the chapel was purchased by Judge Smyly and Robert Hanson of Kimberley for £60, in what would appear to have been a rather generous gift to the community. In the same year, the celebrations for Queen Victoria's diamond jubilee took place. There was a children's party at the Institute and general merrymaking in the village, part sponsored by Judge Smyly, who was living at Watnall Hall and who organised other fund-raising activities for the Institute. It seems hard to disagree with the conclusion reached by Gwen Shaw in her booklet on the chapel, that the building became known as the "Victoria Institute" from about this time, and the plaque on the front would appear to confirm this.

In 1927, Lady Maude Rolleston, together with a group of other ladies, founded the Watnall Victoria Women's Institute and she was its first president. Her husband was already a Victoria Institute trustee and, in 1928, ownership of the Institute passed outright to the WI. Lady Maude and other WI members became its first WI trustees and the building has been in the hands of the WI ever since.

In 1940, the building experienced a brief period of further change when it was commandeered for military purposes. It became part of the rapidly expanding RAF presence in Watnall (see later). In fact, it became No. 12 group's first plotting station. A gallery was built round the inside, overlooking a large plotting table below, which was used to track aircraft movements. A few years later, in 1943, the facility was transferred to a purpose-built bunker across the road and the old chapel took on more mundane duties within the RAF. It was returned to the WI in 1946/7.

7 Education

Before the Education Act of 1870, schooling for poorer children was ad hoc, and provided mainly by the voluntary subscription, or charity schools. These were funded mainly by donations from wealthier people. Watnall had such a school: the Bog End Charity School, built by the Rolleston family in 1752. It still stands, just before the climb up to Greasley Church. These wealthy people often required schools to follow a particular religious line and the Rollestons were no exception. Part of a printed copy of the original foundation document is still in existence. The trustees were required to employ "a schoolmaster or mistress for teaching eight poor children, boys or girls, whose parents belong to the Parish of Greasley". Provision was also made for the payment of "two shillings and sixpence on Christmas Day to each of the said poor children, provided that they shall have regularly attended church on Sundays and Christmas Day, unless prevented by sickness or lameness". By 1832, the school catered for about 20 pupils, but education nationally was on the march, and religious affiliation was to become a political hot potato.

By early in the 19th century, two important groupings of the charity schools had crystallised out. The British Schools was the first, chiefly supported by wealthier Nonconformists. Not to be outdone, the Church of England formed its own group, known as the National Schools, and many larger settlements nearby had both types (Kimberley and Eastwood for example had both British and National schools).

In 1870, the Gladstone Government's Education Act came along. It was greatly significant in that it was the precursor of the present universal system, establishing for the first time the right of all children to an elementary education. It did this by setting up locally elected bodies called school boards, whose job was to fill in the considerable gaps left by the existing voluntary school system. The Boards were funded from rates and required the attendance of all children.

In 1880, the records indicate a major disturbance in Watnall's civic tranquillity. At a meeting in August of Greasley School Board, it was unanimously decided that steps be taken to provide additional school accommodation in Kimberley. The Education Department was attempting to incorporate future provision for both the Watnalls in this project and specified that the new site should be in "proximity of Kimberley but in the direction of Watnall". After numerous changes of policy, this specification seems to have been disregarded and the board school was eventually built at the top of Factory Lane, but in the meantime a hornets' nest seems to have been stirred up in Watnall itself. In November 1880, the ratepayers got a petition together which voiced their disaffection in no uncertain terms. They "learnt with regret that it is the intention of the Greasley School Board to build a group of schools in the hamlet of Kimberley to accommodate 360 children". They pointed out that "If the schools are erected at Kimberley, as proposed, they will be of no practical use to the inhabitants of (Watnall) on account of the distance". They stressed that they would have to bear an equal share of the expense of providing the schools, and urged the Privy Council on Education not to sanction the project. It's not entirely clear what happened to cool Watnall tempers, but the residents' concerns seem to have been addressed in some way, and the deal for the Factory Lane site eventually closed in late 1881.

Sometime later, in 1883, at a meeting of Greasley School Board, the subject of enlarging the Boys School at Beauvale was under consideration. This was because the Rolleston School in Watnall had closed, putting pressure on existing facilities. It can only be assumed that the opening of Factory Lane in 1883 relieved the problem, because in 1885 the clerk to the Greasley Board wrote that "All children of school age (In Watnall) are at the present time attending schools either at Kimberley, Beauvale, or the adjoining parish of Hucknall, the residents of some parts of Watnall being conveniently situated for attending schools in the latter parish." The Watnall ratepayers must have been tolerably satisfied with this situation too, as a year later the clerk confirmed that there had been "no complaints" in respect of attendances at existing schools. On 12th Jan 1892, the Charity Commissioners authorised the trustees of the Rolleston Charity to sell the school, thus ending an era spanning nearly 150 years.

8..Watnall Hall

Watnall Hall was Watnall's stately home, and unfortunately it is now gone. It was, for most of its life, associated with the Rolleston family. The family was a branch of that which originated in Rolleston, Staffordshire, and came to Watnall in the late 16th century. Ralph Rolleston, 2nd son of James Rolleston esq of Lea, Co. Derby, married, "in the time of Queen Elizabeth", Margaret, elder daughter and co-heir of Sir Richard Bingham of Watnall Chaworth, by Anne his wife, and thus acquired the manor of Watnall Chaworth. Watnall continued as the seat of the Rollestons until recent times. The family acquired other premises in nearby Nottinghamshire parishes, and just over the county border in Derbyshire, as well as an estate in Lincolnshire, and at various times also held lands in Middlesex, Staffordshire and Suffolk.

The original house is said to have been started sometime in the early part of the 16th century but note the previously mentioned early reference to a manor house in Watnall Chaworth. In 1446 the house was home to the Binghams and refined enough to have had an "oratory" (private chapel) which was also quite possibly on this site. Many alterations and additions were made over the years, and major rebuilding took place, probably in the early 1700s, during the reign of Queen Anne when the family was at its zenith.

The grounds were entered via the main drive, guarded by a lodge on the corner of Trough Lane, which still exists. In front of the lodge building were the famous wrought iron gates, thought to be the work of Huntingdon Shaw, who produced them at about the time of the last major reconstruction of the hall in 1690. Shaw died in 1710.

Sir Lancelot and Lady Maude – the last of the Watnall Hall Rollestons. Sir Lancelot was born in 1847, the son of an MP who couldn't afford to live at the hall himself and supplemented his income by leasing it out. This is a recurring theme of the Rolleston family; owing to the relative paucity of their estates they frequently couldn't afford to live at their own seat.

Lancelot senior died in 1862, and the policy of leasing the hall continued under his son, who appears to have moved back in, at least temporarily, by 1881, with a small staff. He married in 1882, at the age

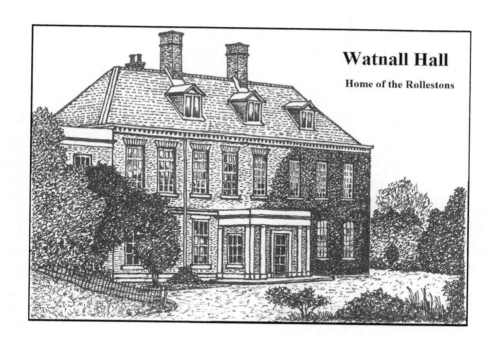

Watnall Hall

Home of the Rollestons

of 35: the lady was Charlotte Emma Maud Dalzeil (Maud). She had considerable wealth and pedigree in her own right, and the marriage brought Lancelot considerable prestige, as well as substantial amounts of money. He became a keen yachtsman and was also a keen huntsman. Although Watnall Hall remained as his "seat" he seems to have leased another property, Edwinstowe House, about two miles from Edwinstowe, probably in the late 1880s.

Lancelot Rolleston was first and foremost a soldier. He joined the Watnall troop of the South Notts Hussars in 1868 and was promoted to Lieutenant Colonel, commanding the Hussars in 1896. The Rollestons are well remembered for their exploits in the Boer War. Colonel Rolleston first went out to South Africa in 1900 at the age of 53 and regarded it as both an adventure and career pinnacle. Lady Maud followed him overseas and established a convalescent hospital for gentlemen. The Colonel was badly wounded in 1900, and it was for his assistance during this incident that Trooper Joe Haywood apparently earned himself the tenancy of the Queen's Head back in Watnall. Lady Maud managed to reach her husband after considerable adventures of her own and the Colonel recovered slowly, but for him the war was over and the Rollestons returned to Watnall in late 1900.

The Rollestons both took a considerable interest in public affairs. Sir Lancelot founded a Scout troop in Watnall; he became chairman of Notts County Council and served as a JP. Lady Maud founded a Girl Guides troop, and a Sunday school at Watnall Hall. She became a magistrate and was a founder member and first president of the Watnall Women's Institute.

Sir Lancelot Rolleston died in 1941. Most of the hall was requisitioned for use as an officers' mess by the RAF during the war, but Lady Maud continued to live there in a few rooms on the first floor. After the war the building was used by the Hollygirt Girls' Boarding School until 1954. Lady Maud continued to live there until she died in 1949.

After 1954, the building stood empty. The main heir of the Rollestons was Miss Dayrell who still owns farms and fields in Watnall to this day. The hall was auctioned in 1954 and bought by a firm of builders who intended to turn it into flats. It proved to be unsuitable and after long wranglings and many problems it was demolished in 1962.

9 Miscellaneous Matters: Inns, the RAF and the Weather Centre

The Royal Oak. The older part of the building seems to have originated as a roadside inn, sometime after the construction of the turnpike road in 1758. The inn is noted in trade directories from 1832, in which Elizabeth Raven is recorded as innkeeper. The Raven family remained here for many decades and appear in trade directories right up to the early years of the 20th century. Shaw's map of 1853 records Elizabeth Raven as innkeeper, occupying the original building, some small gardens and a pigsty. Curiously, a pinfold is recorded on the opposite side of the road, still there in 1880. The adjoining building to the south is divided into four tenements with gardens, occupied by four different people. Two plans survive showing the rather large, Victorian extension to the inn, drawn up for Earl Cowper in 1888/9, built on the site of the tenements to the south. They show an original brew-house, a corn store, and stables. Earl Cowper's crest can still be seen on the front of the extension, as it can on many of the buildings in Watnall. The inn was purchased by Hanson's Brewery from the Desborough Trustees in 1915, after the breakup of the Cowper estates.

The Queen's Head. The inn is mentioned in Rolleston family deeds dating from 1755, which actually concern the holding later known as Chaworth Farm. The farm, discussed previously, was originally owned by the Everingham family and included the present site of the inn. The Rolleston deeds describe the progressive break up of Chaworth Farm by the heirs of the Everingham family, and the inn itself receives a first mention in 1801. It appears as a parcel called "the Old Queen's Head and closes", the "Old Queen" being Queen Anne, and a year or two later, in 1815, it was sold to Edward Gething, a farmer from Brinsley. By 1853, Lord Melbourne had acquired most of the rest of Chaworth Farm, including the smithy, which lay to the south of the inn. The inn itself was acquired by Lancelot Rolleston in 1870, and both the Smithy and Chaworth Farm were purchased by Rolleston in 1915, when he consolidated his holdings following the breakup of the Cowper estates.

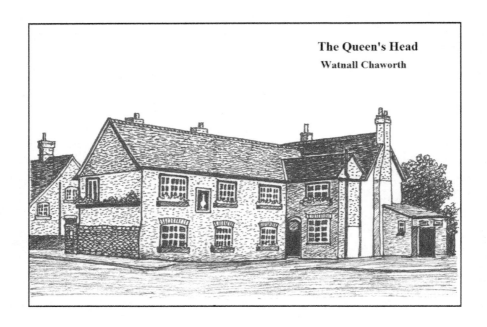

The Queen's Head
Watnall Chaworth

The building is much altered, and the majority dates from the 18th and 19th centuries, although it is possible that there were earlier buildings on the site. Its major development as an inn seems to follow the familiar pattern. The turnpike road, set up in 1758, meant more travellers, and more travellers meant increased demand. The current lounge area probably represents an extension of the original building towards the turnpike road.

In 1851, the landlord at the Queen's was Thomas Jackson, whose family were also heavily engaged locally as blacksmiths and wheelwrights. By 1871, the proprietor was George Watkinson, and by 1881 it was Charles Gilbert. In 1906, Joe Haywood took over, probably the most famous of the inn's landlords. In earlier times, trooper Joe Haywood had what later turned out to be a great stroke of good luck in the Boer War, when he helped to rescue a badly injured Colonel Rolleston. The tenancy of the Queens Head appears to have reflected Colonel Rolleston's gratitude in the matter.

The Wheatsheaf Appears in trade directories from about 1830. It was on the Ivy Farm site, and quite possibly arose as a beer house under the 1830 Act. This was a misplaced attempt to eliminate spirits, particularly gin, from the prevailing working-class menu. Licenses were for six days, for beer and cider only, and quite cheap. A good number of farms set up, selling beer as a side line, and many later became fully licensed inns. Very little information about the Wheatsheaf appears to have survived.

The RAF and the Weather Centre. The RAF arrived in Watnall shortly before the outbreak of the Second World War. They were already established on their airfield at Hucknall and expanded into Watnall to build a control and administration HQ for Fighter Command no 12 group. The group covered a vast area of Britain: the Midlands, Norfolk, Lincolnshire and North Wales. Construction was started in 1938, but it wasn't till late 1940 that the new headquarters became fully operational.

The site straddled both sides of the B600. Airmen's barrack blocks, storage buildings and a junior officers' quarters were to the west of the road and included a good deal of accommodation built in the grounds of Watnall Hall. Also on this side was the Victoria Institute, commandeered for RAF purposes at the beginning of the war. On the east side were the officers' mess, headquarters offices, an underground operations block which was about 60ft below ground level and is now flooded, and a second operations block. This second operations block, called the filter block, was built as a "bunker" on the site of the old Midland Railway station which closed in 1917. It wasn't completed until 1943 and remains an interesting building to this day. Originally a corridor running round three sides opened onto a balcony which overlooked an area containing a large plotting table. These became very well known to the public in war films from the era.

The whole site was, needless to say, top secret and performed a vitally important national role in the war effort. No 12 Group HQ moved to RAF Newton in 1946 and the operations block closed. RAF Watnall itself closed in 1961. The filter block was left in a state of readiness, but it became vandalised and years of neglect and decay took their toll. In the 1980s the building was taken over by the Kimberley Rifle Club.

The RAF recorded the weather at Watnall, and a weather centre was operational on the site since the early 1940s. After the war it remained with the Ministry of Defence, largely for air traffic control purposes, but with a decreasing RAF function in the late sixties it became a civilian meteorological establishment. It formed one of seven similar facilities: the others being London, Southampton, Manchester, Newcastle,

49

Glasgow and Bristol. It changed its name to the "Nottingham Weather Centre" in 1977, apparently because "no one outside the Nottingham area knew where Watnall was". In 1983 a new weather centre was planned on the site; the new buildings being positioned in front of the old ones.

In relatively recent times Watnall has hosted a number of light industrial users, attracted no doubt by its convenient location next to a major Midlands city, and close to the hub of the motorway network.

Of these, the most venerable is probably the bakery. Banchard's first arose in Kimberley when Ernest Blanchard moved into a shop at no 6 James Street. In the early 1950s increasing demand resulted in the move to Watnall.

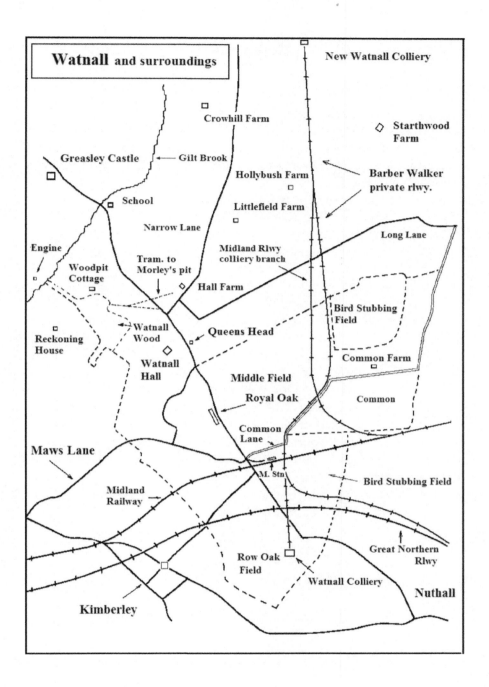

Watnall and surroundings

New Watnall Colliery

Crowhill Farm

Starthwood Farm

Greasley Castle — Gilt Brook

Hollybush Farm

Barber Walker private rlwy.

School

Littlefield Farm

Narrow Lane

Long Lane

Engine

Midland Rlwy colliery branch

Tram. to Morley's pit

Woodpit Cottage

Hall Farm

Bird Stubbing Field

Watnall Wood

Queens Head

Reckoning House

Common Farm

Watnall Hall

Middle Field

Common

Royal Oak

Maws Lane

Common Lane

Midland Railway

M. Stn

Bird Stubbing Field

Great Northern Rlwy

Row Oak Field

Watnall Colliery

Nuthall

Kimberley

51

References

This booklet builds upon a foundation of earlier work, but also incorporates considerable primary material, held at a number of different archives. The author is always willing to assist those with a detailed interest, and a summary of source material has been produced entitled 'A Watnall Collection'. The following general works have been used and are singled out for particular mention.

Watnall Nottinghamshire – A Short History - Roger Hadfield 1985.
Booklet 'From Methodist Chapel to W. I. Hall' by Gwen Shaw'.
Watnall Hall and the Rolleston Family - R.A.Horton.
Griseleia in Snotinghscire - Rodolf Baron Von Hube.
The Antiquities of Nottinghamshire – Thoroton.
The series of volumes 'Kimberley in Old Picture Postcards' by A. Plumb.
The Great Northern Railway in the East Midlands - Alfred Henshaw.

I am greatly indebted to Don Webb, and Roger Grimes for assistance and support in a wide variety of historical matters; also to Paul Anderson for some of the illustrations used. The front cover photograph is reproduced by kind courtesy of A P Knighton and the internet photographic portal   www.picturethepast.org.uk. I would also like to thank my wife Sylvia for assistance in tracking down some of the more obscure references. All contributions, comments, corrections and criticisms will be gratefully received.

About the Author

J M (John) Lee. Born Leicester, England. Educated in Leicester and briefly at the University of Wales. He lived for a short period in the North of England, followed by a spell as a radio officer in the Merchant Navy and afterwards a long career in telecommunications. He has lived for a large part of his later life in Nottinghamshire, England and spent a good deal of time researching local history there. This has resulted in a series of local histories based in the Nottinghamshire area, most of which are published by Amazon..

There is also a novel: The Bombay Rifleman's Chest; a somewhat irreverent but, hopefully, amusing tale from the largely bygone world of 1980s industrial Britain.

Printed in Great Britain
by Amazon

82014045R00031